RUSSIAN PROVERBS

NEWLY TRANSLATED

WITH ILLUSTRATIONS BY
ALDREN WATSON
FOR THE
PETER PAUPER PRESS
Mount Vernon · New York

Like every people, the Russians have their own accumulation of proverbs. Sometimes they sound like our own salty English or American proverbs, sometimes they exhibit that distinctively Slavic flavor of bitter humor in a minor key.

Since our Russian diplomatic visitors have made a habit of flavoring their speeches with such home grown wisdom, we now make this collection available — for those who want to quote from the Russian in rebuttal, or who just want to get the feeling of a nation from its deepest folk sources.

THE CHURCH is near but the road is all ice; the tavern is far but I'll walk very carefully.

No love so hot but marriage cools it.

His fingers took the kopeck, but his back took the beating.

When you take an eel by its tail or a woman by her word, there's precious little stays in your hand.

A horse-dealer never trusts himself — he always calls on God.

Easier to manage a sack full of fleas than one woman.

They are teeth, even though they eat nothing but pudding.

You never get change from a priest, or remnants from a tailor.

A husband's fist leaves no bruise.

You cannot see the spark in flint; you cannot see the soul in men.

Great is Holy Russia, but the sun shines elsewhere too.

A woman is an evil no household should be without.

You can't talk to a judge empty-handed.

Better go to sea in a leaky boat than trust a woman with a secret.

His purse screams when he pulls it from his pocket.

Where the needle goes, the thread follows.

Misers die, and their children empty the chests.

Make yourself into a sheep, and you'll meet a wolf nearby.

Honor is on top of his tongue, and a knife is under it.

It's a waste of time to steal from a thief.

Trust in God, but take care of your garden.

If we knew beforehand where we were going to fall, we could lay down a carpet.

At law the nobleman is always in the right when a peasant brings the suit.

A woman's hair may grow long, but her common sense stays short.

That money-lender would tear the skin off a flea.

Live a hundred years, learn a hundred years — still you die a fool.

Beat your wife with the butt-end of an axe: if she falls to the floor and cries, she is fooling you — give her some more.

The belly is ungrateful — it always forgets we already gave it something.

With loose firewood around, even the priest will steal.

If you drink you die; and if you don't drink you die: so it's better to drink.

Since when does the fiddle pick the tune?

The priest never waits his turn at the mill.

Put your foot in the courtroom — put your hand in your pocket.

The Volga is a good horse; it will carry anything you put on it.

The moon is the Cossack's sun.

The Russian is clever, but it comes slowly — all the way from the back of his head.

Russians do not fear the cross, but they fear the club.

The shortage will be divided among the peasants.

The priest wants more parishioners, but he wants more funerals too.

Counting other people's money will never make you rich.

Don't worry: you can't die before your death.

When you live close to the grave-yard, you can't weep for everyone.

The sea is the fisherman's farm.

When one priest praises another he speaks unclearly — his tongue is in his cheek.

Fear has big eyes.

Officials eat hot food, the people eat cold.

In Moscow they ring the bells often, but not for dinner.

The Russian has three strong principles: *perhaps*, *somehow*, and *never mind*.

Fools shoot, and God directs the bullet.

Adam ate the apple, and we men still have toothache from it.

He is a bad thief who steals from his neighbor.

The hop-vine reaches for a pole; the maid for a man.

When the Devil meets a friend, he takes him down below to his house.

Slander, like coal, will either dirty your hand or burn it.

A Cossack may starve, but his horse will be fed.

The bread of strangers can be very hard.

Go before God with a clean heart, before the judge with money.

Long whiskers cannot take the place of brains.

The fox kissed the hen — right down to her tail-feathers.

Drink a glass of wine at dinner, and you steal a ruble from the doctor.

If you're the priest, you must sing the mass.

Wash a pig as much as you like, it goes right back to the mud.

In this country you can't even pick a mushroom without bowing.

You can't drive straight on a twisting lane.

In a fight the rich man tries to save his face; the poor man his coat.

Learn good things — the bad will teach you by themselves.

If you can tickle yourself, you can laugh when you please.

He doesn't have to poke around in his pocket for fine words.

The little one is too small; the big one is too big; the medium one is just right — but I can't get it.

Outside the tavern it is freezing, but inside his money is melting away.

Better bread and water, than cake and trouble.

No apple is safe from worms.

A laughing bride — a weeping wife; a weeping bride — a laughing wife.

After you've had it seven years, you'll know what to do with it.

Hair by hair, you can pluck out the whole beard.

If you don't know how to be a good servant, you won't know how to be a good master.

You can never fill a priest's belly.

When the Devil grows old, he turns monk.

A guest should not have to honor his host; a host should honor his guest.

All the brave men are in prison.

A wife is not an instrument you can hang on the wall when you're tired playing on it.

Neither a judge nor a stomach has to tell you in words what it wants.

Once it's fallen off the cart, it's gone for good.

Defend yourself against the robber with a club; against the official with a ruble.

If fools wore white fur caps, we'd all look a flock of sheep.

The fool makes ropes out of sand.

Once a word is out of your mouth you can't swallow it again.

If you don't crack the shell, you can't eat the nut.

The husband's sin stays at the doorstep; the wife's enters the house.

An ox gets caught by the horn, a man by the tongue.

Walk fast and you can overtake misfortune; walk slowly and it will overtake you.

It's a poor soldier that doesn't dream himself a general.

You can measure your cloth twelve times, but cut it only once.

Every fox brushes his own tail.

Only a fool will make his doctor his heir.

Afraid or not, you will have to face your fate.

Girls, don't worry when you marry — when your husbands start beating you will be time enough.

The cow may be black, but the milk comes out white.

Man is no mushroom — he doesn't grow in a day.

Eat your food, dear guests — otherwise we'll just throw it to the dogs.

If God listened to every shepherd's curse, our sheep would all be dead.

A pot of oats on the fire sings its own praise.

Siberia is terrible, but life there is better than life in Russia.

There are more twistings to a woman than a path in the forest.

Gold is heavy, but it rises to the top.

Even a blind horse can pull the cart, if he is led.

The priest loves the rich man's funeral, the judge loves the rich man's lawsuit.

He went to the courthouse with his best coat on, but he came home naked.

Life is unbearable, but death is not so pleasant either.

It isn't the horse: it's the oats that pull the wagon.

Don't collect straw for your neighbor's roof while your own is leaking.

He has been sent to count the birches in Siberia.

A Cossack isn't a Cossack without a horse.

Once in every gypsy's life he tells the truth; then immediately he regrets it.

He runs from the bear right among the wolves.

Two women make a market, three a fair.

Lord Time never bows to you; you must always bow to him.

When the abbot goes out to the tavern, the monks get drunk in the wine-cellar.

I would gladly go to war, but I grieve for my poor wife.

These fellows will have it soft in the next world: they'll be made devils at once.

It's a sin to go to a wedding and come home sober.

You'll never get a hangover from other people's vodka.

Love your wife like your soul, and shake her like your pear-tree.

Death is not like your brother — you can't argue with *him*.

Live and scratch — when you're dead the itching will stop.

Life is given by God, but it may be taken by a beast.

The road to Siberia is wide; the lane back is narrow.

You may well laugh — you have good teeth.

It is pleasant to watch somebody else thresh corn.

Before a fight two men are boasters; afterwards, only one.

God has many days left — there's plenty of time to work.

Working may be hard, but eating is pleasant.

As the horse remarked: the grass will last our lifetime; and after that, who cares?

The devil pours honey into other men's wives.

Don't take along your own rules when you enter a strange monastery.

When you pick a wife, close your eyes and open your ears.

Wherever God has a church, the Devil opens a chapel.

When you saw wood, dust will fall.

When you die even a tight box will be comfortable.

If the thunder is not loud the farmer forgets to cross himself.

When the priest visits, don't be so pleased: he has come for something.

He doesn't know the worst of life, who hasn't a handsome young widow to wife.

A gold hammer will break down an iron door.

What good is honor on an empty stomach?

If you're a rooster, crow. If you're a hen, shut up and lay eggs.

Birth, baptism, banns, and burial have one thing in common — the out-stretched palm of a priest.

Expensive medicines are always good: if not for the patient at least for the druggist.

Slap your woman before dinner and you'll have to beat her before supper.

Even if Truth is buried in a gold box, it will break out and come to light.

Noblemen make promises, and peasants have to keep them.

Mosquitoes sing over the living — priests over the dead.

The Czar is generous, but his money filters down through many sieves.

A good reputation sits at home, a bad one runs about town.

To teach a fool is as easy as to cure a corpse.

The mouth of the wolf and the eye of the priest: never satisfied.

No need to plant or cultivate fools: they grow everywhere.

Once your daughter is married, fine young bachelors appear like magic.

Care for your clothes from the day the tailor delivers; care for your honor from the day your beard sprouts.

With the lucky man his enemy dies; with the unlucky man his best friend dies.

Wag your tongue as much as you please, but don't wave your gun.

If you are offered gifts, take. If you are offered curses, run.

Marriage is like sneezing — even when you feel it coming you can't stop.

The brave sing in prisons, the stupid sing in churches.

A wife is very dear to her husband twice: the day he marries her and the day he buries her.

If you find a good thing, do not rejoice. If you lose a good thing, do not despair.

Fish seek deeper water, men a better life.

When two dogs fight, let the third keep his distance.

The kopeck thief is hanged, while the thousand-ruble thief is honored.

Don't choose your bride before you choose your broker.

Once in the pack, you may not have to bark — but you must at least wag your tail.

The bullet is a fool — it only hits where there is a hole.

The crow went traveling abroad, and came home just as black.

A promised horse won't pull the cart.

The hunter killed the horse and caught the hare.

You cannot serve one sparrow on twelve plates.

You cannot write in the chimney with charcoal.

Don't look now, but someone is stealing your potatoes.

If I must drown, better the open sea than the village puddle.

The sober man's secret is the drunken man's speech.

There are two fools in every market: one asks too little, one asks too much.

We don't live uphill, but downhill.

He went for wool, and came home shorn.

To the mouse the cat is a lion.

Debt and Misery live on the same road.

The bear dances and the gypsy collects the kopecks.

If you are tired of a friend, lend him money.

Not all who make love also make marriages.

Don't save the egg and lose the hen.

Drink at table, not behind a post.

If you've eaten it Tuesday, don't look for it Wednesday.

The wolf is no comrade for the horse.

In the country of the blind, the one-eyed man is king.

The neighbor's little things always look big.

If the father is a fisherman, the children know the water.

Better the first quarrel than the last.

When the gentlemen fight, the peasants suffer.

Better beneath the old man's beard than the young man's whip.

A dog is wiser than a woman: he won't bark at his master.

Betwixt life and death: not room for a flea to jump.

When we sing, everybody hears us; when we sigh, nobody hears us.

Though you are turned away at the front door, try knocking at the back with a ruble.

A girl must commit sins, otherwise she has nothing to atone for.

The workman with clean tools is a bad worker.

Old fools are worse than young fools.

The bullet is no respecter of fine uniforms.

A man and a dog belong outdoors; a woman and a cat belong indoors.

After your head is cut off, you won't cry over your hair.

The wife rules the husband not with a stick but a temper.

The rich would have to eat money, but luckily the poor provide food.

When an old crow croaks, listen well.

When the sheath is broken, you cannot hide your sword.

You can jump out of a saddle, but you're stuck fast to a wife.

When the fox sleeps he dreams of chickens.

The paper is still while the pen is writing.

A handsome cage doesn't feed the bird.

The more you complain, the longer God lets you live.

I escaped from a bear in the woods, and ran into my mother-in-law at home.

The Czar isn't fire, but get too close and you'll be burnt to death.

When the parish priest goes to the country for a visit, the devil comes to town.

If you fear the wolf, keep out of the forest.

As proud as an eagle, as brave as a hen.

In calm weather even women can steer the boat.

Pray to God, but keep rowing to shore.

Presents are cheap, true love is dear.

When the wolf asked the goat to dinner, the goat declined with thanks.

His thoughts are over the mountains; danger is over his shoulder.

Make peace with men and make war with your sins.

The mare was making friends with the wolf, but somehow or other she didn't come home.

Death is blood brother to the Russian soldier.

If you feast the guest you must feed his dog.

Even the doorstep of the rich finds itself embarrassed by the poor.

A good millstone will grind any grain; a bad millstone will grind itself away.

The body belongs to the Czar, the soul to God, the back to the Squire.

Who has not known the sea has not known sorrow.

Happiness and health go out by hundredweights and come back by ounces.

In this world not everyone with a long knife is a cook.

He is so mean you can't borrow snow from him in Winter.

The bashful beggar oft goes away hungry.

When dogs bark, wind carries the sound away.

With God you may cross the sea; without him, do not cross the door-step.

Seven never wait for one.

The future is his who knows how to wait.

When the Devil himself has failed, he sends a woman.

You can't smell lemons with a pig's snout.

One soldier does not make a whole regiment.

The water is up to his neck, and he's asking for a drink.

Every one loves the tree that shelters him.

Better to turn back than lose your way.

It fits — like a saddle on the cow.

Jealousy and Love are sisters.

Only when the wolves are fed will the lambs be safe.

Dry straw should keep out of reach of fire.

You can't skin the same carcass twice.

The worst wheel groans the most.

With some people even their roosters seem to lay eggs.

It's not your business to rock your neighbor's cradle.

Don't sell without praising, don't buy without belittling.

Better to trade at a loss than steal at a profit.

Marry a wife who can read, and she'll find all the holidays on the calendar.

Even Spring has no delight in a strange land.

If you have no devil in your house, take a son-in-law.

Only tailors go without clothes and shoemakers without shoes.

The seller has one price, and the buyer quite another.

He is young, but he has read old books.

My hands and feet are my tormentors — but my belly God preserve.

The greatest Czar is put to bed at last with the same shovel.

When the wolf shows his teeth, he isn't laughing.

Bury memory like a stone in water —
only a bubble or two will show.

There is a cover for every pot.

So long as the sun is out, who asks for
the moon?

Man does what he can; God does
what he will.

An untried friend: an uncracked nut.

Where there's honey there will be
flies.

What goes in with mothers' milk
goes out only with the soul.

Strong as Samson was, even he could
not lift a ruble from an empty purse.

Truth keeps silence when money
talks.

Hens shouldn't crow like roosters.

When the Governor takes up his pen, peasants pray and birds fall silent.

Put a light load on a donkey, and it thinks it can lie down.

With a good wife and enough cabbage soup, don't look for more.

Better beg than steal, better work than beg.

You'll never catch an old wolf in an old trap.

The old dog can't eat his bone, and won't let others near it.

A girl's modesty lasts only till you get her over the doorsill.

A pot of luck is better than a sack of wisdom.

If you eat cherries with lords, they will spit the stones at you.

You can't sew buttons on your neighbor's mouth.

Better your own crust than your neighbor's pie.

The law is like a sleigh: a clever judge can steer it either way.

When the thief prays to God, the Devil steals his prayers in flight.

Be friends with the wolf, but keep one hand on your axe.

If there is no apple, eat a carrot.

Lie down with dogs and you'll get up with fleas.

Marry off your son when you will, your daughter when you can.

A woman laughs when she must, and cries when she likes.

Poor lamb: it has seven shepherds.

It's a stupid mouse that knows only one hole.

To every card-sharp there are born seven fools.

Feed the wolf as much as you like, still he looks back to the forest.

Too much butter never spoiled the broth.

He who fears sparrows never plants grain.

Only God guards fools.

Don't praise the wheat until it's in the sack, the squire until he's in the coffin.

In the next world, money-lenders will count red-hot rubles with bare hands.

Ah, you can even get used to Hell.

A spoon of tar will spoil a cask of honey.

You can't die twice, and you can't live but once.

God is too high and the Czar is too far.

Even a sick wolf can handle a lamb.

The beaten dog needs only to see the stick.

The bell calls to church, but never goes inside.

He who is fated for the gallows need not fear the sea.

Even crooked sticks burn straight.

A bad compromise is better than a good battle.

Only the eagle may look into the sun.

When the mouse is full, the bread tastes stale.

Don't ask the ox to take a drink, but to carry the water-buckets.

The first wife comes from Heaven, the second from Earth, the third from Hell.

A good husband is father to his wife.

When a soldier dies, he's too bad for Heaven; and he drinks so much the devils won't take him in Hell.

All Cossacks do not become captains.

Don't spit into the well — you'll be thirsty by-and-by.

When the head is hollow the shins will get hurt.

You can escape a snake, but not a slander.

A full stomach makes a poor student.

You must get down from your neighbor's horse on demand, even in the mud.

The star-gazer's toe is often stubbed.

If you never see new things, you can go on enjoying the old.

The older daughter is married off by her parents, the younger daughter by her sister.

Oppression comes not from the Czar but from his favorites.

They prayed so hard for good weather, God sent them drought.

Don't drive your horse with the whip — use the oatbag.

You don't learn as much from buying as from selling.

When the bachelor dies, not even a dog howls.

Even a foolish wife won't tell her husband the truth.

When you jump the ditch, you risk your neck.

If you want to sell spoiled goods, seek a blind buyer.

Beware the horns of the bull, the heels of the donkey, and the heart of the monk.

We are related: the same sun dries our rags.

Don't hang all you own on one nail.

All that trembles does not fall.

The falling leaf whispers something to living men.

The ikon and the shovel come from the same tree.

If you go to war, pray; if you go to sea, pray twice; and pray three times if you go to wed.

When you sue the Czar, ask God to play the judge.

Never trust the friendship of a joker.

A man without a wife is a man out in January without a fur cap.

When the Czar roars, the axe will fall.

Take the wool, but pray leave the hide.

A bachelor is a goose without water.

It's no fun to travel alone, even if you're shipwrecked and drowned.

A kind word now is better than a pie later.

Give the nut to the beauty, and the rose to the sage.

You can trust him like you can trust ice in late Spring.

Talk in market and you tell the world.

If you own a fur coat you will be plagued by lice.

So long as I have moonlight, the stars can suit themselves.

A goat on the hill looks higher than a cow in the meadow.

An old bridegroom does not stay married long.

Spending is quick and easy, earning is slow and hard.

All girls are good — then where do bad wives come from?

Don't worry if you borrow — only if you lend.

Give your wife too much leeway and you'll steal from yourself.

It's too late to think of wine when the cask is empty.

That one is hard on clothes — she is wearing out her third husband.

Wolves catch others, but then are caught themselves.

One fisherman knows another from afar.

A word is not a bird: once on the wing it can never be caught again.

Between a woman's yes and no, it's hard to fit a needle.

Servants in silk, masters in bankruptcy.

You give nuts to the squirrel when its teeth are gone.

At the bottom of the wine you will always find dregs.

A lamb at home is better than a cow abroad.

Spit in his eye, and he will swear it's holy dew from Heaven.

He aimed at the crow and hit the cow.

A good man is good inside; a good horse is good outside.

There is no good answer to a stupid question.

Straddle two horses, and you'll fall in the mud.

A fortune is not always a friend; but a friend is always a fortune.

Strength and glory are servants of the rich.

No sin to ask, and no calamity to be refused.

Light a candle for the Devil too: you never know.

Where there are no fish, even a crawfish can pass as one.

Though the horse can cross, the hen gets drowned.

He who rushes at life dies young.

Refuse free wine : it will cost you less to buy it.

The hand that takes never tires of its work.

At a fire, water is precious.

Do not guarantee a watch, a horse, or a wife.

Not everyone who snores is sleeping.

On a dangerous road, wear your beard over your shoulder.

Love your neighbor but put up a fence.

Don't bother to be born handsome or good — just be born lucky.

The load is light that rests on someone else's shoulders.

The wolf took pity on the lamb — he
left it its bones and fleece.

A hundred friends are not too many; one enemy is.

Every animal is fond of its own fur.

If you can't find wisdom at home, you won't be able to buy it abroad.

A wise companion cuts the journey in half.

If only one evil woman lived on earth, every man would claim she was his wife.

We are shrewder at sunrise than at moonrise.

If you want to feast on honey, first kill the bees.

If you spit at Heaven, you will dirty your own face.

The bird is small, but the beak is sharp.

The law is straight, but judges are crooked.

A crab is not a fish; a bat is not a bird; a hen-pecked husband is not a man.

Giving a present to the rich is like giving water to the sea.

Pray to God, and don't offend the Devil.

The hungry man can think only of food.

If you ride in his cart, you must join in his song.

The uninvited guest is worse than a Tartar.

A new friend: a frozen stream in Spring.

Big fish swallow little fish, and swallow them whole.

To one man, two enemies together are a regiment.

Ask a lot, but take what is offered.

The strength of the ruble is in the kopeck.

If you offer to carry the basket, don't complain of the weight.

To eat well sit next the hostess; to drink well sit next the host.

Our bodies can stand dinner after dinner, but not blow after blow.

Good porridge was never spoiled by butter.

He bowed when he borrowed from me, I bowed when I collected from him.

You lend money by hand and go after it by foot.

We do not study to learn wisdom but to pass examinations.

The slower you drive, the further you get.

A wife isn't a jug — she won't crack if you hit her a few.

The tears of strangers are only water.

For women to bear children isn't easy, but to keep quiet is really hard.

I see the church; as for the tavern, I'd better ask my way.

If we eat the seed now, we won't have to worry about the crop next year.

He is so mean he tries to skim the cream off mud.

Before you die, first pay the priest.